AF735098

Dominique Smith is a barrister at Deka Chambers, specialising in travel law, inquests, clinical negligence, and personal injury. She has a busy court practice, with a particular interest in cross-border clinical negligence disputes and complex personal injury claims. Dominique is known for her expertise in respect of jurisdictional issues and package travel contracts. She often acts in multi-injury claims in the County Court and High Court, for both claimants and defendants.

Dominique has been recognised as a 'rising star' in travel law for several years in the Legal 500 and is also ranked in Chambers and Partners. She is a co-author of the leading travel textbook, *Saggerson on Travel Law and Litigation*, published in 2022, with this book being her second publication.

A Practical Guide to Cross-Border Clinical Negligence Claims

A Practical Guide to Cross-Border Clinical Negligence Claims

Dominique Smith

Barrister, Inner Temple

Law LLB (First Class Honours), University of Surrey

Law Brief Publishing

Published 2023 by Law Brief Publishing, an imprint of Law Brief Publishing Ltd
30 The Parks
Minehead
Somerset
TA24 8BT

www.lawbriefpublishing.com

Paperback: 978-1-914608-63-6

PREFACE

This book is intended to be a helpful guide for those dealing with cross-border clinical negligence claims. For many practitioners, there isn't a crossover in their practices between clinical negligence work and travel/cross-border work. They are distinct areas in and of themselves. Yet, in dealing with these claims, one must have the ability to understand the complexities of both areas, and that is notwithstanding the fact that these claims are complex in any event. With medical tourism becoming an ever-popular option for individuals, and these claims increasingly landing on our desks, I thought it was an opportune time to write about this topic to assist anyone grappling with these claims. There may be some errors in what follows (despite my very best efforts!) and I will endeavour to iron these out in a next edition, if I am spared. I have sought to state the law as of 2nd January 2023.

I also thought this was an appropriate place to write some expressions of thanks. As a pupil barrister, I was introduced to cross-border work by my then supervisors, Jack Harding and Andrew Spencer. I vaguely remember looking at them with some horror when given a piece of cross-border work to look at, as I had no clue about package travel claims or the like, let alone jurisdiction. Both spent a lot of time teaching me everything there was to know, and never wavered in their kindness in sparing an extra half an hour to explain something to me. Surprisingly, they saw something in me and supported my tenancy application. Once I was qualified tenant, Sarah Prager KC also took me under her wing. She has been a huge support, answering my queries at all hours and providing me with guidance and great friendship as I have navigated my early years at the Bar.

To Jack, Andrew, and Sarah – I owe an enormous thanks. I will always be grateful to each of them for the impact they have each had on my life and career.

Secondly, I wish to thank my Mum, Dad and sister who have been with me every step of this journey, and to whom I owe so much. A page is not enough to thank them for the sacrifices they each made to help get me to the Bar.

Finally, I wish to say thank you to Tim and Garry, who saw potential in me to write this book. Without them, it wouldn't exist!

I hope you all find this an insightful read.

Dominique Smith
2nd January 2023

CONTENTS

CHAPTER ONE

INTRODUCTION

In recent years, it has become increasingly common for people to undergo cosmetic procedures, of both the surgical and non-surgical kind. Not only is cosmetic surgery no longer a taboo, but it is now often actively celebrated, with individuals charting their progress following surgery on TikTok and Instagram to their followers around the globe.

What has sparked this trend? Undoubtedly, social media has played a large part. It proliferates in our lives in a way unlike ever before, with an increasing emphasis on displaying a perfect life, and a perfect appearance, to the outside world. Celebrities from reality TV shows may endorse foreign providers of dental or surgical treatment online, to demonstrate how easy (and cheap) it is to look like a star. Photographs can be manipulated and edited using photo-altering technology or filters, which allow individuals to see how they may look through a different lens. Yet, whilst we can edit our photos to eliminate our perceived flaws, the only way to physically change our appearance is via surgical and/or non-surgical means.

In recent years, the option of travelling abroad for a cosmetic procedure has become an attractive one. Often, treatment abroad is advertised at a much cheaper price than in the UK and can be booked to take place relatively quickly. Rather than wait months or even over a year for surgery in the UK, it can be booked in a matter of weeks abroad. The surgery is often presented as a holiday where individuals can stay in a luxury hotel whilst they recover. Adverts sometimes show patients enjoying the beach and the culture of the place in which they are staying once they are discharged. On social media and on clinic websites, previous patients may share their success stories and experiences to emphasise that any patient from the UK will be in safe hands. There may also be an option to see a surgeon from abroad in the UK on a 'roadshow', to have any questions answered prior to surgery, or the clinic themselves may advertise themselves as catering specifically to a British audience.

But what if things go wrong?

Whilst the number of people seeking treatment abroad appears to have increased, so to it seems have the number of cross-border clinical claims. Reports of poor surgery and deficient aftercare abroad have begun to surface in the news and are starting to fill our desks. Unfortunately, so have reports of individuals dying either during, or shortly after, their cosmetic procedures. In late 2022, the Foreign and Commonwealth Development Office ("FCDO") issued advice for tourists considering medical, surgical, or dental treatment in Turkey. It noted that 22 British nationals had died in Tukey since January 2019 following medical tourism visits. The FCDO advised individuals to refer to a specific website for a list of medical providers who were approved by the Turkish Ministry of Health.[1] One can only assume that the FCDO will continue to monitor the number of British nationals dying from surgery abroad. It remains to be seen whether the FCDO goes further, issuing advice in respect of other countries who offer medical tourism.

Should an individual, or indeed an estate, wish to bring a claim in respect of a poor surgical/treatment outcome or a death abroad, it is far more complicated than in a claim where the negligence or breach of contract occurred in England or Wales. The following chapters are

---

1 https://www.gov.uk/foreign-travel-advice/turkey/health (accessed in January 2023).

intended to provide a guide as to how to navigate these claims from an early stage in litigation.

CHAPTER TWO

DEATHS ABROAD AND INQUESTS

When an individual dies abroad following a cosmetic procedure, questions will naturally arise as to how the deceased came by their death. If they died during or shortly after the procedure, why did it happen? What caused their death? Were they fit and well before the procedure, or are there concerns that they were never a suitable candidate for surgery to begin with? Are there records substantiating a timeline of what happened and when? If not, why not? These are undoubtedly questions that will be in the forefront of any family's mind.

To begin with, investigations will need to be undertaken to establish as clearly as possible the circumstances surrounding the deceased's death. The investigations and their outcomes will be of importance to any family members, potential claimants, and indeed potential defendants. Any investigations will inevitably provide material relevant to any later inquest and/or civil claim but can take a significant period of time to complete, which may result in some delay to later proceedings.

Investigations following the death

A number of investigations may be commenced following the death of an individual abroad. Most commonly, the police in the relevant jurisdiction may open an investigation to establish how the deceased died. This may involve the medical practitioners involved being interviewed or later prosecuted, or there may be scrutiny over the treatment records available. In some cases, the investigation may unfortunately be lacking, leaving the family of the deceased with a number of unanswered questions.

A criminal investigation abroad can bring with it some difficulties. The investigation and any subsequent criminal proceedings that follow in that jurisdiction can sometimes take a significant amount of time. If the family of the deceased are considering bringing proceedings in the courts of England and Wales relating to the death, this can pose issues in respect of limitation. It is therefore pertinent for practitioners to consider at an early stage what the applicable law relevant to any civil claim may be[2], so that decisions can later be made as to whether proceedings should be protectively issued. For example, if it appears that the claim will be governed by Turkish law, rather than English law, practitioners will need to investigate the limitation period under Turkish law for contractual and/or tortious claims so that the claims (when brought) are not out of time. If this is not considered at the earliest stage of litigation, the limitation period could expire before relevant investigations are completed, leaving a claimant in a difficult position.

Post-mortems and repatriation

If the circumstances surrounding the cause of the deceased's death are unclear, a post-mortem will usually be arranged in the country where the death occurred. It is important to bear in mind that local laws in each jurisdiction will differ, thus it may well be the case that a post-mortem can occur without the permission of the next of kin, or that organs and tissue from the deceased can be retained. Further, toxicology and other test results may not be available in advance of the

2 See Chapter Six for a detailed discussion of applicable law.

body being repatriated, which can result in some delays to deciphering the deceased's cause of death. If a post-mortem is carried out abroad, the report itself (when provided) may require translation and costs may need to be incurred to obtain a translated version.

A family may wish for the deceased's death to be investigated by a coroner in England and Wales, particularly if they are unsatisfied with the local investigations in the country of death, or the standard of the post-mortem report from the country of death. A coroner in England and Wales is under a duty to investigate a death abroad if the body of the deceased is returned to their area and if the circumstances are such that an investigation would have been conducted if the death happened in England and Wales.[3] Those circumstances in which a coroner must commence an investigation into a person's death are set out in section 1(2) of the Coroners and Justice Act 2009, namely if a coroner has reason to suspect that:

- the deceased died a violent or unnatural death;
- the cause of death is unknown; or
- the deceased died while in custody or otherwise in state detention.

If the family of the deceased wish for the death to be investigated by a coroner in England and Wales, not only must the death fall within section 1(2) of the Coroners and Justice Act 2009 to engage the coroner's duty to commence an investigation, but the deceased must not have been buried abroad or cremated. This is because the body of

3 *R v HM Coroner for West Yorkshire ex parte Smith (no 1)* [1983] QB 335. For further discussion on a coroner's jurisdiction to hold an inquest following a death abroad, see *Shafi v Her Majesty's Senior Coroner for East London* [2015] EWHC 2106 (Admin).

the deceased must be within the coroner's area for an investigation to be conducted.[4] If the body of the deceased is not in the coroner's area, or if there is no longer any body following a cremation abroad, it is highly unlikely that any investigation by a coroner in England and Wales (and subsequently any inquest) could ever take place. Consequently, should a family wish to contact their local coroner's office with regards to a possible investigation into the deceased's death, arrangements will need to be made for the body to be repatriated.

Repatriation can only occur once the investigations in the relevant jurisdiction have been concluded. As such, a local death certificate will need to be obtained (if issued) once the death has been registered in that country. This again may require translation. In addition, in some jurisdictions, a form of release is required for repatriation to take place. It is important to check what the local requirements are in the country of death when considering repatriation, again to prevent further delays in the coronial process at home.

Prior to repatriation taking place, the body is usually embalmed. Following repatriation, a coroner may organise for a further post-mortem to take place. However, any post-mortem may be affected by the embalming processes that have already taken place, thus the examination may not be as thorough as it could have been (and indeed may be more limited) had no embalming processes taken place.

Following the post-mortem, the coroner's investigation must be discontinued if the cause of death becomes clear (albeit this will not occur if there remains a reason to suspect that the deceased died a

---

4 Coroners and Justice Act 2009, section 1(1).

violent or unnatural death or died in custody/state detention) and the coroner does not think it is necessary to continue the investigation.[5]

The listing of an inquest

If the coroner does not discontinue their investigation, an inquest into the death will be listed. Inquests concerning deaths abroad often bring with them an additional layer of complexity, in that relevant documentation and witnesses are usually located abroad. Whilst a coroner will make every effort to obtain information from abroad, there may come a point when the evidence hoped for is still lacking and there would be no useful purpose in deferring the hearing of the inquest any further.[6]

That said, with the involvement of lawyers representing the parties, efforts can be made by interested persons to obtain documentation from their clients to assist in the coroner's investigation, and families can make submissions as to what documents (such as medical records and the like) they consider should be made available.

Can difficulties arise in an inquest where a death has happened abroad?

An example of the difficulties that may arise in an inquest concerning a death abroad can be seen in *Shafi v Her Majesty's Senior Coroner for East London.*[7] In *Shafi*, the deceased was a British national, who was holidaying in Dubai at the Burj al Arab Hotel. Following an argument

5 Coroners and Justice Act 2009, sections 4 and 6.

6 See *Shafi v Her Majesty's Senior Coroner for East London* [2015] EWHC 2106 (Admin), paragraphs 27-35.

7 *Shafi v Her Majesty's Senior Coroner for East London* [2015] EWHC 2106 (Admin).

with a chambermaid on 7th April 2011, he was arrested and taken into custody. He was thereafter placed in solitary confinement and was found dead during the evening of 12th April 2011. The deceased's body was brought back to the East London coroner's area and the coroner assumed jurisdiction to inquire into his death. The deceased's cause of death was unknown. During the course of the coroner's inquiries, the coroner sought information from the Dubai authorities through the Foreign and Commonwealth Office.[8] All items requested were forthcoming, except for details of any CCTV footage from the scene. No CCTV footage or stills were ever produced for the coroner. During the inquest itself, no witnesses from Dubai were called to give live evidence. The coroner gave reasons for his decision to read the statements of those witnesses under Rule 23 of the Coroners (Inquests) Rules 2013, namely that he considered there was "*good and sufficient reason to believe the maker of the written evidence will not attend the inquest hearing... they are not compellable*".

An application was subsequently brought by the deceased's mother for the inquest conclusion to be quashed and for a fresh investigation and inquest to be ordered, raising complaints concerning the insufficiency of the inquiry in relation to the CCTV footage, as well as in relation to the evidence being admitted under Rule 23.

In respect of the CCTV footage, the applicant's complaints were not accepted by the court. Notably, Lord Justice Bean stated that: "*there is only so much that a coroner can do to obtain evidence from a foreign state, however friendly. The coroner has no power to investigate overseas, send investigators overseas, or require police to investigate overseas. Nor*

8 Now known as the Foreign, Commonwealth & Development Office.

can the coroner compel the disclosure of documentation from the overseas country or compel witnesses from the country to attend to give evidence".[9]

However, the applicant's complaints as to Rule 23 were upheld. The coroner did not explain what good and sufficient reasons there were, other than there had been some discussions with the authorities in Dubai. No detail was provided as to what those discussions were, nor whom they were with. It was not explained (or indeed clear) whether the witnesses were willing to attend, or whether the state did not wish for them to attend. It is therefore unsurprising that the court considered that the coroner could have invited the witnesses to attend in person, or alternatively, via video link.[10]

Shafi indicates that whilst a coroner should exercise the tools at their disposal to obtain relevant information from abroad, such as by contacting the relevant local authorities and the like, the inability to obtain that evidence will not be a barrier to the holding of the inquest. As a coroner cannot compel disclosure of documentation from abroad, the evidence in the coronial investigation could unfortunately paint an incomplete picture into the deceased's death.

Giving evidence remotely

Should it be proposed that a witness be called to give remote evidence from abroad at an inquest, consideration should be given as to whether there are any legal complications preventing the witness from doing so. It cannot be assumed that a witness giving evidence from another

---

9 See paragraph 26.

10 Rule 17 of the Coroners (Inquests) Rules 2013 allows for witnesses to give evidence at an inquest via a video link.

jurisdiction to an English court can do so without consequence. It may not be permissible, or indeed may be illegal, to do so.

Take the example of a coronial investigation into a death of a British national in a hospital in Antigua. A witness statement has been obtained from the operating surgeon about the circumstances of the deceased's death, and the coroner and the family of the deceased would like the surgeon to be called to give live evidence at the inquest. However, it is proposed that the surgeon gives evidence from Antigua, due to his clinical commitments. Checks would thereafter need to be made with the FCDO to see if there is any objection at a diplomatic level to the witness giving evidence via remote means to an English court. It may be that permission needs to be obtained from the local courts in Antigua, so that the surgeon can give his evidence from abroad.

For those interested persons whose witnesses are located abroad, it may be useful to consider at an early stage in advance of the inquest whether such permission is needed, so that any evidence in relation to permission being granted is available to the coroner at the pre-inquest review. Without checking with the FCDO whether the witness can give evidence from abroad, a coroner is unlikely to permit them to give their evidence orally via video link. Checking whether permission is required with the FCDO is a straightforward task: one simply needs to email or telephone the office.

Prevention of Future Death Reports

At the conclusion of the inquest, a coroner may proceed to make a Prevention of Future Death Report ("PFD"). The coroner's duty to make a PFD is triggered where anything revealed by the investigation into the deceased's death gives rise to a concern that circumstances creating a risk of other deaths will occur, or will continue to exist, in the future, and that action should be taken to prevent this.[11] It is important to bear in mind that the PFD does not need to be restricted to matters causative to the death and is not restricted to those persons or organisations who reside in England and Wales, nor is it restricted to interested persons only. Should a coroner proceed to make a PFD, a response must be provided by the individual/organisation subject to the PFD within 56 days of the date on which the report is sent.[12]

For those acting for the family of the deceased, a coroner may decide to invite submissions as to the family's views on PFDs, and whom, if anyone, these should be addressed to. If a PFD is made against a clinic or hospital, or if the coroner has made findings in their conclusion about the medical care the deceased received (e.g., blood tests were not performed), these may be pleaded in the particulars of any civil claim. That said, an inquest is not a vehicle to build a civil claim.

For those acting for interested persons in relation to a cosmetic surgery or treatment death abroad, it is pertinent to consider at an early stage what matters are likely to give the coroner concern about the risk of future deaths (if there are any), and what steps have been taken to prevent any further deaths. This may assuage the coroner's concerns such that a PFD is not necessary. Documentary evidence may be required to assuage any such concerns, which may demonstrate lessons that have been learned or steps that have been taken to prevent another death occurring in similar circumstances. That evidence should be provided to the coroner as soon as possible in their investigation.

---

11 Coroners and Justice Act 2009, Schedule 5, paragraph 7(1).

12 Coroners (Investigations) Regulations 2013, regulation 29(4).

CHAPTER THREE

PACKAGE TRAVEL CLINICAL NEGLIGENCE CLAIMS

Where a contract for surgical or dental services may exist, it is vital from the outset to determine whether the contract could be argued to fall within the Package Travel and Linked Travel Arrangements 2018 ("PTR 2018"), or alternatively, whether the contract is a consumer contract.[13] These questions are central to understanding who the potential defendants are (if you are for a claimant), issues of jurisdiction, and the applicable law and/or standards of the contract. This chapter specifically deals with those claims that can be considered to fall under the PTR 2018.

PTR 2018 – is it a 'package' or a 'linked travel arrangement'?

It is not uncommon to see businesses advertising surgical or cosmetic/dental treatment deals abroad, which include accommodation and flights. What businesses may not realise is that the combination of services provided may amount to a regulated package holiday under the PTR 2018.

For claimants, these claims are often easier to handle if there is a regulated package in existence. What may help matters is that a clinic or surgical provider may directly advertise on social media or on their website that they offer 'packages' for sale. For defendants, it is crucial to consider from the outset of the litigation process if the treatment

[13] Consumer contracts are dealt with in Chapter Four of this book.

contract is caught by the PTR 2018, as undoubtedly, businesses may not realise they have sold a package and may not be appropriately insured to meet a claim. If the business in question is not aware that they have sold a package, it is likely that they will not have complied with the insolvency and bonding provisions of the PTR 2018.[14] A breach of these provisions can carry criminal sanctions, that defendant lawyers will need to ensure their clients are aware of.

To determine whether the contract can be deemed a 'package' or a 'linked travel arrangement', one must first look at the PTR 2018. The PTR 2018 applies to packages sold after 1 July 2018. If a package was sold prior to 1 July 2018, it is likely governed by the previous regulations, namely the Package Travel, Package Holidays and Package Tours Regulations 1992, which are not dealt with within this book.

A package is defined at Regulation 2 of the PTR 2018 as the following:

- A combination of at least two different types of travel services for the purposes of the same trip or holiday, if:
    - Those services are combined by one trader, including at the request of/in accordance with the selection of the traveller, before a single contract on all services is concluded; or
    - Those services are:
        - Purchased from a single point of sale and selected before the traveller agrees to pay;

[14] See regulations 19 to 26 of the PTR 2018.

- Offered, sold or charged at an inclusive or total price;
- Advertised or sold under the term "package" or a similar term;
- Combined after the conclusion of a contract by which a trader entitles the traveller to choose among a selection of different types of travel services; or
- Purchased from separate traders through linked online booking processes.[15]

A linked travel arrangement is defined at Regulation 2(3), as:

- At least two different types of travel service purchased for the purpose of the same trip or holiday, not constituting a package, resulting in the conclusion of separate contracts with the individual service providers, if a trader facilitates:
    - On the occasion of a single visit to, or contact with, a trader's point of sale, the separate selection and separate payment of each travel service by travellers; or
    - In a targeted manner, the procurement of at least one additional travel service from another trader where a contract with such other trader is concluded at the latest 24 hours after the confirmation of the booking of the first travel service.

---

15 For further detail, see the Package Travel and Linked Travel Arrangements 2018, regulations 2(5) and 2(6).

the European Council and European Parliament had in mind when creating the Directive did not include surgical or dental treatment (hence the reason why they are not mentioned in the Directive) and that tourist services should be limited to those services inherently linked to travelling, such as tours and the like.

A claimant may point to a treatment provider's website or social media accounts, which may explicitly refer to their services as medical tourism. It may also be suggested by a claimant that medical tourism is, by its very nature, a tourist service. In addition, if the Directive considers that spa treatments (which are not entirely dissimilar to some cosmetic treatments) could be a tourist service, this shows a wide reading of the phrase 'tourist service' should be undertaken, such as to encompass cosmetic treatments.

Pertinently, there is no current higher English or Welsh authority as to the definition of a tourist service. It can only be a matter of time before the courts are tasked with grappling with this issue, given its importance in determining the legal framework governing these cases.

Liability under the PTR 2018

Regulation 15 of the PTR 2018 provides that "*the organiser is liable to the traveller for the performance of the travel services included in the package travel contract, irrespective of whether those services are to be performed by the organiser or by other travel service providers*".[21] To determine whether a potential defendant is an organiser, one must look to Regulation 2.

Regulation 2 defines an organiser as "*a trader who combines and sells, or offers for sale, packages, either directly or through another trader or*

[21] Package Travel and Linked Travel Arrangements 2018, regulation 15(2).

together with another trader"[22], or the trader who transmits the traveller's data to another trader in accordance with paragraph (5)(b)(v). If a package has been sold by a particular provider, it is difficult to see how they will not fall within the definition of an organiser.

Contracting out of the package

A potential defendant, such as a clinic or business, may seek to raise the argument that they were merely acting as an agent and are therefore not subject to the PTR 2018. There may be a stipulation in the treatment contract to state that the defendant has an agency arrangement with the treatment provider and that they do not accept any liability for negligence or breach of contract.

However, this is a risky argument for a defendant to raise, as the PTR 2018 specifically caters for this situation. Regulation 30 stipulates that any declaration that the organiser or trader is acting exclusively as a travel service provider, or as an intermediary or in any other capacity, or any declaration that the package or linked travel arrangement does not constitute a package or linked travel arrangement, does not absolve that organiser or trader from the obligations imposed upon them under the PTR 2018. Even if the contractual agreement stipulates that the traveller waives or restricts their rights under the PTR 2018[23] or

22 Package Travel and Linked Travel Arrangements 2018, regulation 2(1).

23 Package Travel and Linked Travel Arrangements 2018, regulation 30(2) stipulates that a traveller may not waive any right granted to them under the Regulations.

attempts to circumvent the PTR 2018 in any way, this will not be binding on the traveller.[24]

From a claimant practitioner's perspective, the suggestion that a clinic or business was solely acting as an agent can be rebutted by way of regulation 30(1). On the other hand, defendant practitioners should check the treatment contract to see if any such term exists, so that they can provide appropriate advice to their clients that this will not prevent the package falling within the PTR 2018.

Bringing a claim under the PTR 2018

If the claim is caught by the PTR 2018, it will likely be governed by English law.[25] As such, liability, causation, and quantum will be determined in accordance with English law. It is not uncommon therefore for a claimant to plead breaches of the terms of the Consumer Rights Act 2015 with regards to the contractual relationship. A discussion of the applicable standard of care in these claims can be found at Chapter Seven of this book.

Is the potential defendant insured?

Even if the claimant has a viable claim under the PTR 2018, the potential defendant/s in question may not have any insurance to meet the claim. This is not an uncommon problem in these claims. Claimant practitioners should investigate at any early stage whether

---

[24] See Package Travel and Linked Travel Arrangements Regulations 2018, regulation 30(3).

[25] See Article 6(1) of Regulation EC No 593/2008 on the law applicable to contractual obligations (Rome I), which Chapter Six of this book discusses in further detail.

the potential defendants have insurance to meet the claim, as a claimant may otherwise later be in a position where any judgment against the defendant will remain unsatisfied.

CHAPTER FOUR

NON-PACKAGE CONTRACT CLINICAL NEGLIGENCE CLAIMS

A potential claimant may establish that they have a contract between themselves and the treating foreign practitioner and/or foreign clinic yet may find that they cannot avail themselves of the PTR 2018. This may arise where the claimant did not purchase flights or accommodation from the treatment provider, such that they do not have a qualifying package under the PTR 2018. They may, however, be able to seek redress under the consumer contract provisions under the Civil Jurisdiction and Judgments Act 1982. Previously, prior to Brexit, consumers could rely upon the provisions set out in Brussels Recast[26], however this is no longer applicable to post-Brexit claims.

Consumers under the Civil Jurisdiction and Judgments Act 1982

The Civil Jurisdiction and Judgments Act 1982 defines a consumer as "*a person who concludes the contract for a purpose which can be regarded as being outside the person's trade or profession*". In *Flowers v Centro Medico & Berkley Espana (t/a Hospital Clinica Benidorm)*[27], the court (when looking at the definition of a consumer under Article 17 of

[26] Regulation (EU) No 1215/2012 on jurisdiction and the recognition and enforcement of judgments in civil and commercial matters (recast), specifically Article 17.

[27] *Flowers v Centro Medico & Berkley Espana (t/a Hospital Clinica Benidorm* [2021] EWHC 2437 (QB).

Brussels Recast) considered that Mrs Flowers, who was a patient at a Spanish hospital, would have fallen within the definition of a consumer had she survived. Provided there is no suggestion the treatment is linked to the person's trade or profession, a claimant will usually have no difficulties in asserting that they fall within the definition of a consumer, similar to Mrs Flowers.

However, problems may arise when a person's trade or profession is closely linked to their appearance. Take the example of a claimant who is an Instagram beauty influencer. The claimant may decide to undergo surgery abroad to maintain their appearance, which, for a number of reasons, may unfortunately go awry. If the claimant proceeds to bring a claim in the English courts, the foreign surgeon/clinic defendant may argue that the claimant's surgery was not outside of their trade or profession, because the claimant's appearance is part and parcel of their profession. They may suggest that the claimant's image is directly correlated to their business, so as to render the claimant to fall outside the definition of a consumer.

For those acting for a claimant whose image may correlate to their work, it is important to bear in mind that it will likely be challenged by a defendant that the claimant is a consumer in those circumstances, and the claim could potentially fail at the first hurdle. For those acting for defendants, it is crucial to analyse at an early stage whether the claimant's treatment can truly be said to be outside of their trade or profession, as a defendant may wish to raise an argument in this respect.

Both parties can look to certain factors in each case to help determine this issue, such as whether the treatment was tax deductible, or whether the claimant posted about the treatment on their social media platforms to generate income.

Defining a consumer contract

A consumer contract is defined as a contract which has been concluded with a person who "*(i) pursues commercial or professional activities in the part of the United Kingdom in which the consumer is domiciled, or (ii) by any means, directs such activities to that part or to other parts of the United Kingdom...*"[28] But what does it mean to 'direct' activities to the UK?

Pammer v Reederei Karl Schlüter GmbH & Co KG; Hotel Alpenhof GesmbH v Heller[29] provides some helpful guidance. In this case, the ECJ said there must be clear evidence that the trader manifested an intention to establish commercial relations with consumers from other member states, including the domicile of the consumer. The following features were deemed to constitute evidence of an activity "directed to" a member state[30]:

- The international nature of the activity at issue, such as certain tourist activities.
- Mention of telephone numbers with the international code.
- Use of a top-level domain name other than that of the member state in which the trader is established, e.g., ".de" or ".com".

28 Civil Jurisdiction and Judgments Act 1982, Section 15E(1).

29 *Pammer v Reederei Karl Schlüter GmbH & Co KG; Hotel Alpenhof GesmbH v Heller* [2011] 2 All ER (Comm) 888.

30 Ibid, see paragraph 83. The ECJ set out that the above list is not exhaustive.

- The description of itineraries from one or more other member states to the place where the service is provided.

- Mention of international clientele composed of customers domiciled in various member states, in particular by presentation of accounts written by such customers.

In addition, if a website permits consumers to use a different language or a different currency, the court held that this can be taken into consideration and can constitute evidence from which it may be concluded that the activity has been directed to England and Wales. Whilst not specifically discussed in *Pammer*, if the treatment provider organises roadshows (with consultation opportunities) in England and Wales, these too can arguably demonstrate that the defendant's activities have been directed to the United Kingdom.

If you are acting for a claimant and pleading that a consumer contract is in existence, it is pertinent to plead features of the contract that indicate that the activities were directed to England and Wales. On the other hand, if you are acting for a defendant and the evidence of any direction of activities is lacking, then it may be possible to challenge that a consumer contract is in existence.

Deceased Consumers

A situation may occur where an individual, who would have qualified as a consumer[31], passes away before litigation commences. An estate may therefore wish to bring a claim on a deceased consumer's behalf. A question may arise as to whether the estate can plausibly argue that

[31] For further information regarding the definition of a consumer, see Section 15B of the Civil Jurisdiction and Judgments Act 1982.

the deceased's right of action as a consumer passed to the estate upon their death.

This is a question that was considered in the case of *Flowers*.[32] In that case, Mrs Flowers, a 67-year-old woman, was admitted to a private hospital facility in Benidorm, Spain on an emergency basis. Whilst her health insurance covered her emergency admission, there was no such cover after her initial admission. Nine days after her admission, she died in that facility from multiple organ failure, as a consequence of contracting sepsis. The claimants (namely the deceased's husband and various other family members) pursued a claim against the clinic, Centro Medico, and Centro Medico's public liability insurer on the basis that Centro Medico was at fault for Mrs Flowers' death. The claimants argued that the deceased was a consumer and would have been entitled to utilise the jurisdictional gateway under Article 17 of Brussels Recast to bring the proceedings. The claimants further argued that the deceased's right of action passed to her husband and heirs, who subsequently had the same entitlement to use the jurisdictional gateway as consumers under her contract. The defendants contested jurisdiction and the entitlement of the claimants to use the jurisdictional gateways pursuant to CPR 11. In his judgment, HHJ Graham Wood QC did not consider the deceased's heirs could pursue her consumer claim through the same jurisdictional gateway. The Judge noted that a route for the heirs through the consumer gateway was "*totally unprecedented*" within European jurisprudence, as it would open the floodgates for potential claimants as the estates and heirs of contracting parties in a way that could not have been intended when the legislation was put in place.

32 *Flowers v Centro Medico & Berkley Espana (t/a Hospital Clinica Benidorm* [2021] EWHC 2437 (QB).

Flowers is not a decision that bodes well for consumer claims involving the estate of the deceased. However, it is a pre-Brexit case, concerning Brussels Recast. *Flowers* could be challenged by claimants on the basis that it is only a first instance decision, and that the United Kingdom has now Brexited. However, a defendant may suggest that no different outcome arises post-Brexit and *Flowers* should bite nonetheless.

CHAPTER FIVE

JURISDICTION

Establishing that the courts of England and Wales have jurisdiction to deal with a cross-border clinical negligence claim can be a thorny issue. It is often an issue that is contested by defendants, and indeed, a claimant who wishes to bring proceedings in England and Wales may be usurped in doing so by a defendant in their own jurisdiction. The issue of jurisdiction should not be looked at lightly by either claimant or defendant practitioners, and it should not be assumed that the English and Welsh courts will always have jurisdiction to hear these claims.

How is jurisdiction established?

In order to establish jurisdiction, the burden of proof is on the claimant to prove that the claim passes through a jurisdictional gateway. It is for the claimant to show that they have the 'better of the argument' on the material available before the court.[33] If the evidence before the court is uncertain or insufficient, such that a judge may not

---

33 *Brownlie v Four Seasons Holdings* [2017] UKSC 80 para 7 affirmed the position in *Goldman Sachs v Novo Banco* [2018] UKSC 34, para 9. See further *Alta Trading Limited v Bosworth* [2020] EWHC 2757 (Comm), where Sir Michael Burton stated: "*if [the court] decides that the claimant has the better of the case, he will have a good arguable case or a plausible evidential basis. If the defendant has the better of the case then the claimant fails*".

be able to reach a conclusion as to which party has the better of the case, it will suffice if the claimant has a plausible evidential basis.[34]

Rule 6.37 of the Civil Procedure Rules ("CPR") sets out three stages that the court must consider when considering whether to allow service of proceedings on a foreign defendant and to exercise its jurisdiction to hear the claim. Notably, the claimant must satisfy the court of the following:

- That there is a good arguable case that the claim against the foreign defendant falls within one of the jurisdictional gateways set out at paragraph 3.1 of Practice Direction 6B.

- In relation to that foreign defendant, that there is a serious issue to be tried.

- In all the circumstances, England is clearly or distinctly the appropriate forum for the trial (*forum conveniens*) and the court ought to exercise its discretion to permit service of the proceedings out of the jurisdiction.[35]

Should a claimant not meet the above factors, the court will decline service on the foreign defendant and decline exercising its jurisdiction.

---

[34] *Alta Trading Limited v Bosworth* [2020] EWHC 2757 (Comm) para 13.

[35] See further the commentary at 6.37.13, 6.37.14, 6.37.15, 6.37.16 in Volume I of the White Book.

Good arguable case

As set out above, the jurisdictional gateways are set out in Practice Direction 6B, specifically at paragraph 3.1. In cross-border clinical negligence claims, the relevant gateways are usually the following:

- Claims in relation to contracts where the contract:
  - was made within the jurisdiction; or
  - was made by or through an agent trading or residing within the jurisdiction; or
  - is governed by English law.
- Claims in tort where:
  - damage was sustained, or will be sustained, within the jurisdiction; or
  - damage which has been or will be sustained results from an act committed, or likely to be committed, within the jurisdiction.

Often, in cross-border clinical negligence claims, there will be claims in both contract and tort. By way of an example, a contractual claim may exist against a clinic or surgical/dental provider, and a separate claim may exist against the surgeon themselves in tort. It is important to clearly distinguish each of the claims and to consider whether jurisdiction can be established in any or all of them.

In terms of the contractual gateways, it is straightforward to establish jurisdiction in a package clinical negligence claim, as the claim is usually governed by English law.[36] In a non-package contractual claim, the issue is somewhat more complicated. Can it be demonstrated that English law applies to the contract? If not, are there arguable grounds to demonstrate that the contract was made within this jurisdiction, or by or through an agent trading or residing within this jurisdiction? Should a claimant not be able to demonstrate these factors, the claim is unlikely to pass through the contract gateways.

Turning to the tort gateways, in *Brownlie II*[37] the Supreme Court favoured a wider reading of the word 'damage', noting that Lady Hale had observed in *Brownlie I*[38] that "*if I am seriously injured… the pain, suffering and loss of amenity which I suffer are all part of the same injury… the damage is in a very real sense sustained in the jurisdiction*". Consequently, damage is not limited to direct damage and in most cases can be argued to have been sustained in the jurisdiction of England and Wales when an individual returns home from treatment abroad.

Serious issue to be tried

In demonstrating that there is a serious issue to be tried, the claimant must show that there is a real, rather than a fanciful, prospect of

---

36 See Chapter Six for further information.

37 *FS Cairo (Nile Plaza) LLC v Lady Brownlie (as Dependant and Executrix of Professor Sir Ian Brownlie CBE QC)* [2021] UKSC 45 (SC).

38 *Four Seasons Holdings Incorporated v Brownlie* [2017] UKSC 80 (SC).

succeeding in the claim.[39] The merits test is the same as when a claimant resists summary judgment.[40]

Forum conveniens

The key case that all practitioners should be aware of when considering forum conveniens is that of *Spiliada Maritime Corp v Consulex Ltd (The Spiliada).*[41] Two questions arise when considering forum conveniens:

- Has the claimant established that England and Wales is "*clearly the appropriate forum for the trial of this action*"?

- If not (and the court is satisfied that there is prima facie another forum which is more appropriate for the trial of the action), has the claimant satisfied the court that there are special circumstances by reason on which the trial should nevertheless take place in this country?[42]

Each case will be fact sensitive as to whether there are circumstances to render the courts of England and Wales the more appropriate jurisdiction to hear the claim. Matters such as the complexity of the

39 *Altimo Holdings and Investment Ltd v Kyrgyz Mobile Tel* [2011] UKPC 7; [2012] 1 WLR 1804.

40 See further the commentary at 6.37.15 in the White Book, Volume I.

41 *Spiliada Maritime Corp v Consulex Ltd (The Spiliada)* [1987] AC 460 (HL).

42 See *Harty v Sabre International Security Limited (formerly SIS Iraq Limited) and another* [2011] EWHC 852 (QB), in which Mr Justice Macduff cited *The Spiliada.*

applicable law[43], the location of witnesses, and the impact this may have on the trial[44], may point a court to conclude that England, or indeed another forum, is the appropriate jurisdiction. Giving an example, if the applicable law is Polish law, almost all of the witnesses and experts reside in Poland, and the negligence itself happened in Poland, a court may consider that Poland is more likely to be the appropriate forum than England.

Challenging jurisdiction

Unless a defendant challenges jurisdiction, they will be deemed to have submitted to the jurisdiction by participating in the proceedings. A defendant can challenge jurisdiction by utilising the Part 11 procedure set out in the CPR. It cannot be stressed enough how important it is for defendants wishing to contest jurisdiction to follow the procedure set out within Part 11, otherwise a jurisdictional challenge may not get off the ground.

At first, the defendant must file an acknowledgment of service.[45] Within 14 days of filing the acknowledgment of service, an application under Part 11 disputing the court's jurisdiction must be made and must be supported by evidence.[46] If a defendant does not

43 *Pike v Indian Hotels Company Limited* [2013] EWHC 4096 (QB), [2013] 12 WLUK 744.

44 *Stylianou v Masatomo Toyoshima & Suncorp Metway Insurance Limited* [2013] EWHC 2188 (QB), [2013] 7 WLUK 740.

45 Civil Procedure Rules 1998, rule 11.1(2).

46 Civil Procedure Rules 1998, rule 11.1(4).

file an application within 14 days, they will be treated as having accepted that the court has jurisdiction to try the claim.[47]

Service of proceedings

One of the preliminary issues that practitioners will need to grapple with is that of service of proceedings. First, it must be determined whether proceedings can be served within the jurisdiction or whether they need to be served outside of the jurisdiction, and whether permission of the court is (or is not) required. Most often in these claims, proceedings will usually need to be served outside of the jurisdiction on the foreign defendants and an application will need to be made in respect of the same.

If a defendant does need to be served out of the jurisdiction and the permission of the court is required, CPR 6.37 sets out what an application for permission must set out. When considering the application, the court will consider the factors above, which have already been discussed at some length. If the claimant fails in establishing that the claim passes through a jurisdictional gateway and that the claim has real prospect of success, jurisdiction will not be established.

A recent case concerning such an application is that of *Pal v Damen*, which provides some useful insight into how the court approached this issue.[48] In *Pal*, the claimant was a UK national domiciled in England. In May 2016, she underwent elective cosmetic breast implants at a clinic operated by the second defendant in Belgium ("the clinic"). The surgery itself was carried out by the first defendant, a

47 Civil Procedure Rules 1998, rule 11.1(5).

48 *Pal v Damen* [2022] EWHC 4697 (QB).

consultant plastic surgeon ("the surgeon"). It was alleged by the claimant that the surgery was performed negligently, such that she subsequently suffered personal injuries and losses. The claimant issued proceedings against both the surgeon and the clinic, advancing her claim in both contract and tort. Both defendants contested jurisdiction, however it was accepted by all parties that Belgian law was the applicable law of the tort/contract. The application contesting jurisdiction came before Master Cook.

To succeed in establishing jurisdiction, the claimant had to prove that she had an arguable case against both defendants. The key issue in this case was which of the defendants she had contracted with (or indeed whether she had in fact contracted with both). When considering this issue, the court was presented with evidence of the terms and conditions on the clinic's website. The terms and conditions stated that "*physicians are liable for any damages suffered by a patient...*" and that the clinic could not "*be held liable, under any contractual and/or non-contractual clause whatsoever, for damage resulting from a medical accident that occurs during the procedure...*" The clinic produced a witness statement to confirm that the claimant would have seen the terms and conditions on the website, and subsequently would have had to tick to indicate she had read them when requesting a consultation. However, the height of the claimant's evidence was that she could not recall seeing or approving any such terms and conditions. Expert evidence was obtained by the parties in support of their respective positions. The claimant's and surgeon's experts were of the view that the claimant entered into an 'all-in contract', which meant that the claimant had a contract exclusively with the clinic that made a commitment to take care of everything, rather than two distinct contracts with the clinic and surgeon. The experts reached this view, notwithstanding the fact they acknowledged the claimant had read the terms and conditions and had appeared to accept them. The clinic's expert, however, reached the view that there were two separate agreements. The clinic's expert concluded that the agreement between the clinic and the surgeon rendered the surgeon responsible for any damage resulting from a medical accident occurring in a procedure. Due to deficiencies in both the claimant's expert report and the surgeon's expert report, Master Cook concluded that the claimant could not show that she had a good arguable case that there was a contract for treatment with the clinic and her arguments in respect of jurisdiction against the clinic therefore failed. Notwithstanding that, she was able to demonstrate that she had a good arguable case for the existence of a contract between herself and the surgeon, meaning that the courts in England and Wales did have jurisdiction over that claim.

The Italian Torpedo

Practitioners should be aware of the 'Italian Torpedo', which could be utilised in these claims. The Italian torpedo refers to a tactic that may be utilised by potential foreign defendants, in which the foreign defendant issues proceedings or seeks a negative declaration in their home court prior to the claimant issuing proceedings in England and Wales, to seize jurisdiction. As an example, a claimant may send a letter of claim to a potential foreign defendant, outlining the case they will be bringing against that defendant in the English courts. That foreign defendant may then seek a declaration from a court in their local country that they are not liable in respect of any allegations of medical negligence put forward by the claimant. The purpose of this is simply to frustrate the claimant's claim.

Prior to Brexit, Articles 29 to 31 of Brussels Recast[49] provided that where proceedings involving the same cause of action and the same parties were brought in the courts of different member states, the

[49] Formally known as Regulation (EU) No 1215/12012 on jurisdiction and the recognition of judgments in civil and commercial matters (recast).

courts other than the court first seised must stay the proceedings until the jurisdiction of the first court is established. An example of what used to happen pre-Brexit is as follows. A claimant wishing to bring proceedings in England and Wales following negligent dental surgery in Turkey would send a letter of claim to the Turkish dental surgeon and clinic, outlining the case they were going to bring in the English courts. Upon receiving that letter of claim, the Turkish dental surgeon and clinic may turn to seek the assistance of the Turkish courts in obtaining a negative declaration, namely that the claimant's allegations against them have no basis. At that stage, the claimant would not have had an opportunity to issue proceedings in England and Wales, as they were simply following the relevant pre-action protocol in sending a letter of claim. Even if the claimant thereafter decided to issue proceedings in England after the defendant sought a declaration in the Turkish courts, the English courts would likely stay the proceedings. The result of this was that a claimant could sometimes be put in a position where they would have to fight a claim in Turkey, rather than in their home courts, as they may not be able to establish jurisdiction. Further, there would be considerable logistical and costs consequences if the claim was heard in another jurisdiction, as very few jurisdictions have rules regarding recoverable costs that are as advantageous to claimants as in England and Wales.

Since the UK departed from the EU, Brussels Recast no longer applies to proceedings commenced after 1st January 2021. Consequently, common law rules now apply.

Post-Brexit, a defendant may ask the English courts to stay proceedings where there are simultaneous actions pending in England and a foreign country between the claimant and defendant that concern the same, or similar, issues.[50] This may arise where again, in

[50] This is otherwise known as lis alibi pendens.

a similar situation, a defendant seeks a negative declaration from a foreign court.

However, the implications of Brexit now mean that the fact that a negative declaration is being sought in a foreign court by a defendant will not in and of itself determine whether the courts in that jurisdiction are the appropriate forum rather than England and Wales, so as to render a stay of proceedings in England and Wales appropriate. In *De Dampierre v De Dampierre*[51], Lord Goff referred to the principles in *The Spiliada*[52] and said that the court would ordinarily grant a stay if the court concluded that there was another available forum which was clearly more appropriate for the trial of the action, but that the same principle was applicable whether or not there were other relevant proceedings already pending in an alternative forum.[53] Despite that, the existence of those proceedings may, depending on the circumstances, be relevant to the inquiry.[54]

What can practitioners take away from this? In essence, the Torpedo is no longer strong post-Brexit. Just because a negative declaration is sought in a foreign court does not mean that the English courts will simply stay the proceedings and allow the matter to be dealt with in the foreign courts. What once was a potential tactic for defendants in respect of jurisdiction will no longer have the same effect.

---

51 *De Dampierre v De Dampierre* [1988] AC 92 (HL) at [108].

52 *Spiliada Maritime Corp v Consulex Ltd (The Spiliada)* [1987] AC 460 (HL), as referred to above.

53 For further discussion, see *The Abidin Daver* [1984] AC 398 (HL).

54 Ibid.

CHAPTER SIX

APPLICABLE LAW

When bringing a cross-border clinical negligence claim, it is vital to determine what the applicable law is to the contract and/or tort. If a claim is brought both in contract and in tort, it is worth bearing in mind that the applicable law may not be the same in respect of both causes of action. It is crucial for both claimant and defendant practitioners to turn their minds to the question of the law applicable to the claim at an early stage, as issues in respect of limitation may transpire later down the line.

How do you determine the law applicable to the claim?

To determine the law applicable to the claim, reference must be made to the following regulations:

- *Rome I – Regulation EC No 593/2008 on the law applicable to contractual obligations.*

- *Rome II – Regulation EC No 846/2007 on the law applicable to non-contractual obligations.*

As indicated from the above, Rome I only applies to contractual claims and Rome II only applies to tortious claims. It is important to note that these regulations are still applicable post-Brexit.

Rome I

In a contractual claim, practitioners should initially look to Article 6 of Rome I. Article 6(1) provides that where a consumer contract exists, the contract shall be governed by the law of the country where the consumer has their habitual residence, provided that the professional:

- pursues his commercial or professional activities in the country where the consumer has their habitual residence, or

- by any means, directs such activities to that country or to several countries including that country, and

- the contract falls within the scope of such activities.

However, a caveat to the above exists at Article 6(4). Article 6(4) states that Article 6(1) will not apply to a contract for the supply of services where the services are to be supplied to the consumer exclusively in a country other than that in which they have their habitual residence.

In a claim where a regulated package of surgery or treatment exists under the PTR 2018, a flight will often be supplied to the consumer in their country of residence. As at least one flight will take place in the country where the consumer habitually resides, there should be no difficulty in a claimant suggesting that Article 6(4) does not apply, as the services are not exclusively being supplied outside of their country of residence. Provided the above criteria are satisfied (which they almost always are in a package claim), the applicable law in such a scenario would be English law.

The position however in respect of a consumer contract claim is more complicated. Taking the example of a clinical negligence claim where there is a contract for both surgery and accommodation, both of those services will be supplied exclusively in a country *other* than the consumer's habitual residence. Consequently, Article 6(4) would apply, rendering Article 6(1) inapplicable.

In that scenario, practitioners may therefore have to look to Article 3 of Rome I (which refers to freedom of choice of law). Article 3(1) states that a contract shall be governed by the law chosen by the parties. It states that "*the choice shall be made expressly or clearly demonstrated by the terms of the contract or the circumstances of the case*". It is therefore essential to look closely at the contract itself, as it may stipulate that the applicable law is Polish law, for example. On occasion, the consent form may present itself as a quasi-contract and refer to jurisdiction and applicable law in relation to any potential claims arising from the said treatment. However, it is not uncommon in these claims for no formal written contract to be in existence.[55] Often, various exchanges take place on social media, or via email communications or WhatsApp when arranging the treatment, such that there is an arguable issue from the outset of the litigation as to what the applicable law is.

Article 5 of Rome I provides for a situation where Article 3 does not apply (i.e. where the parties have not chosen the law applicable to the contract). Article 5(1)(b) provides that a contract for the provision of services shall be governed by the law of the country where the service provider has their habitual residence. As such, foreign law would apply. There is a caveat however at Article 5(3), which provides that the law of another country will apply where it is clear from all the circumstances of the case that the contract is manifestly more closely connected with a country other than that indicated at Article 5(1). A claimant could therefore utilise Article 5(3) to suggest that English law applies, however there are likely to be significant differences in the position of the parties as to whether the contract could be seen to be manifestly closer connected to England. This may be established

55 For example, in *Clarke v Kalencinski & Ors* [2022] EWHC 488 (QB) the claimant did not sign any contract or document, save for a consent form that was not before the court. Nonetheless, the defendants admitted that a contract existed (see para 77 of the judgment).

where all of the pre-surgical consultations took place in England, as well as any aftercare, and where the treatment facilitators and/or providers are English.

Rome II

In a tort claim, practitioners should look to Article 4 of Rome II. Article 4(1) of Rome II states that the law applicable to a non-contractual obligation arising out of a tort shall be the law of the country in which the damage occurs. This is irrespective of the country in which the event giving rise to the damage occurred, and irrespective of the country in which the indirect consequences of that event occur.

Simplifying this, the general rule is that the law of the tort claim will be that of the country in which the negligent treatment occurred.

There is however an exception to this at Article 4(2), which applies where both the person claimed to be liable and the person sustaining damage both have their habitual residence in the same country at the time when the damage occurs. If that is the case, the law of that country will apply. That said, this is likely not to arise in these cases.

What if there is a contractual claim and a tortious claim?

A claim may be brought in both contract and tort because it is practicable to sue both the clinic and the surgeon/clinician for insurance purposes, or as one may have deeper pockets than the other. In those circumstances, the applicable law for both the tortious and contractual claims may be different.

Nonetheless, practitioners may wish to avail themselves of Article 4(3) of Rome II. Article 4(3) provides that where it is clear from all of the circumstances of the case that the tort is manifestly more closely connected with another country, the law of that other country will apply. For example, if it can be shown that English law applies to the contractual part of the claim against the clinic, it could be argued by a claimant that English law should similarly apply to the tortious claim against a surgeon by way of Article 4(3) as there is a manifestly closer connection with England by way of a pre-existing contractual relationship. This argument may be raised by the claimant as it may lead to a particularly advantageous situation if English law does apply, particularly if English law is more generous in terms of damages than the potentially applicable foreign law. That said, the court will need to examine all of the circumstances of the case to see if there really is a manifestly closer connection with England. The burden is on the claimant to establish that Article 4(1) has been displaced by Article 4(3) and is a high one.

What approach will the court take when issues in respect of Article 4(3) arise?

Winrow v Hemphill[56] is not a cross-border clinical negligence claim, yet it demonstrates the approach the court will take when issues in respect of Article 4(3) arise. In *Winrow*, the claimant was involved in a road traffic accident in Germany, where she sustained injury. She had been living in Germany for many years prior to her accident and continued to live there for 18 months after her accident. She received a significant amount of medical treatment for her injuries in Germany. She was, however, habitually resident in England at the date of the hearing. She had also attended a pain clinic upon her return to England, sought treatment for depression there, and had suffered a loss of earnings. Upon weighing up and comparing these various factors, the court did not consider that the factors demonstrated a

56 *Winrow v Hemphill* [2014] EWHC 3164 (QB).

manifestly closer connection of the tort with England rather than Germany. As such, the law applicable to the claim in tort was German law.

Issues in respect of applicable law

Naraji v Shelbourne[57] is a cautionary tale for practitioners when considering issues of applicable law in these claims. By way of a brief background, the claimant was a professional footballer who had signed for Sheffield United. In 2006, he suffered a rupture of an ACL graft in his knee and sought medical attention from Dr Shelbourne, who practised in Indianapolis. Sheffield United contracted with Dr Shelbourne in respect of the claimant's treatment on the claimant's behalf. The claimant proceeded to undergo an ACL reconstruction, which was performed by Dr Shelbourne in 2006, yet the claimant did not regain full match fitness and consequently did not play professional football thereafter. The claimant sought further treatment from Mr Jari in Manchester thereafter, however the claimant was also dissatisfied with that treatment.

The claimant commenced proceedings against both Dr Shelbourne and Mr Jari both in contract and in tort in respect of the alleged negligent treatment. In his defence, Dr Shelbourne asserted that the applicable law of the claim against him was Indiana law, and the claimant's claim was time-barred. Subsequently, a trial on several preliminary issues was ordered, to consider liability, causation, and whether Indiana law was the applicable law to the claim against Dr Shelbourne (and what the effect of that law was). In terms of the tortious claim, under section 11 of Part III of the Private International Law (Miscellaneous Provisions) Act 1995, the general rule was that the applicable law was the law of the country in which the events

57 *Naraji v Shelbourne* [2011] EWHC 2398 (QB).

constituting the tort occurred. Whilst the claimant attempted to suggest that the relevant question was where the injury manifested itself (i.e. in England), the court disagreed and found that the time and place at which the injury occurred was during the surgery in Indiana. As such, Indiana law applied to the claim in tort. Turning to the claim in contract, the choice of law was governed by the Rome Convention, therefore Indiana law was again the applicable law.[58] Unfortunately for the claimant, this meant that the two-year limitation period under Indiana law applied and his claim in respect of the negligent surgery was time barred. That said, the claimant failed to establish causation in any event.

---

58 For further information, see section 1 of the Contracts (Appliable Law) Act 1990.

irreducible standards in life-threatening situations where local custom, practice and standards are irrelevant, and this was such a situation.[66]

Given the above, there is a real question in these claims as to whether local standards evidence is required when there is a package travel contract in existence. Whether the negligence can be considered egregious, blatant, and life-threatening, such that local standards are irrelevant, is a key issue. It is notable that the claimant in *Clarke* developed severe sepsis in consequence of her surgery and was admitted to the intensive care unit. If the negligence cannot be described in the way as set out in *Lougheed* (such that the position is distinguishable from *Clarke*), it would be safer for claimants to obtain a local standards report discussing the relevant medical standards of care/operation, unless the defendant has contracted to operate to the same standard as a UK surgeon. Where there is no package travel contract, but English law applies, local standards evidence will inevitably be required.

---

66 See further the discussion at paragraph [110] of *Clarke v Kalencinski & Ors* [2022] EWHC 488 (QB).

CHAPTER EIGHT

EXPERT EVIDENCE

As mentioned previously in this book, expert evidence will usually be required in respect of the applicable law to the claim (if foreign law applies), the relevant standard of care[67], and in respect of quantum. This chapter discusses what expert evidence is required in respect of each type of claim, as well as potential pitfalls that practitioners should look out for.

If the claim is governed by English law, what expert evidence do I need?

In a cross-border clinical negligence claim governed by English law, depending on the circumstances of your case and whether liability is in dispute or not, expert evidence may be required in respect of breach of duty of care[68], causation, and condition and prognosis. The claim will operate in a very similar way to a domestic clinical negligence claim in this respect.

If English law applies, but evidence is required in respect of the local standard of care, it is important to ensure that the foreign experts understand specifically what they are asked to advise on. All too often do the courts see local standards reports that discuss local law, rather than applicable standards. If an expert has not understood from their

---

67 However, see Chapter Seven as to the position regarding the relevant standard of care following *Clarke v Kalencinski & Ors* [2022] EWHC 488 (QB).

68 An in-depth discussion of the standard of care, and whether expert evidence is needed on this issue, is set out at Chapter Seven.

instructions what they are being asked to advise on, and proceeds to opine on law rather than standards, it presents a picture that the expert has misunderstood the nature of their role in the proceedings. It may be beneficial to have a conference with the experts at any early stage, to ensure they understand what is required of them and the nature of their role under CPR Part 35.

What expert evidence do I need in a claim governed by foreign law?

In a claim governed by foreign law, expert evidence may still be required in respect of breach of duty, causation, and condition and prognosis, as well as in respect of quantum. It cannot be assumed that a recoverable head of loss in English law will also be a recoverable head of loss under foreign law. That said, there is no reason why the condition and prognosis reports could not be obtained from English experts where foreign law applies.

Expert reports

If foreign law applies, the experts the parties will be relying upon will usually be based abroad and may not have much experience of providing evidence to an English court. As such, there is potential for their evidence to be non-compliant with CPR rule 35. Irrespective of whether you are acting for a claimant or defendant, it is important to have a conference with your experts at an early stage, to iron out any potential issues in their reports and to ensure they are confident with their conclusions.

Pal v Damen gives an example of what can happen when expert evidence in these claims goes awry.[69] In *Pal*, when considering the expert evidence obtained by all three parties in an application contesting jurisdiction, Master Cook noted that the first defendant's expert report was not CPR compliant and that it "*failed to comply with practically every requirement*" of CPR Part 35, such that he ultimately could place no weight on the report.[70] In addition, although the claimant's expert report did comply with CPR Part 35, the court found that parts of the expert's reasoning did not withstand logical analysis.

Pal provides a timely reminder to practitioners to ensure that any expert evidence relied upon not only complies wholeheartedly with CPR 35, but that it also takes full account of the evidence provided to withstand scrutiny. Given that experts in these cases are usually in another jurisdiction, it is important to ensure that they are fully aware of the stringent requirements set out in CPR 35, so as to avoid the court placing little, if any, weight on their evidence.

Wall v Mutuelle – a potential pitfall

Practitioners should be aware of the case of *Wall v Mutuelle de Poitiers Assurances* when dealing with a claim where the applicable law is foreign.[71] Whilst *Wall* may be familiar fodder to those who regularly deal with cross-border claims, for those who do not regularly encounter cross-border work, it is a decision that must be grappled

---

69 *Pal v Damen* [2022] EWHC 4697 (QB). See Chapter Five for a further detailed discussion of the case.

70 See paragraph 56 of the judgment. It was also noted that the expert was acting as an advocate and that he did not fully consider the available documentary evidence.

71 *Wall v Mutuelle de Poitiers Assurances* [2014] EWCA Civ 138 (CA).

with and understood as it rears its head frequently in cross-border clinical negligence claims.

The background facts are as follows. In *Wall*, the claimant suffered serious injuries in a road traffic accident in France. Liability was admitted, thus the only issue between the parties was quantum. When looking at the applicable law, Article 4(1) of Rome II[72] rendered French law the applicable law, which therefore applied to the assessment of damages. Article 1(3) of Rome II stated that the regulations "*shall not apply to evidence and procedure*". The claimant subsequently contended that whilst French law applied, evidence and procedure was governed by English law. The claimant wished therefore to call expert evidence in a number of relevant disciplines. The defendant, however, said this was not appropriate. They argued that the applicable law was French law, therefore the court should order a French-style expert report compiled by a single agreed expert or pair of experts, who would then incorporate into their report any necessary expertise from French medico-legal experts. The Court of Appeal determined that the court was not mandated when trying a case to which foreign law applied to award the same amount of damages a foreign court would award. The court considered that expert evidence it should order fell to be determined by the law of the forum (i.e. England) and that English courts were "*ill-equipped*" to receive expert evidence in the French manner. Further, by allowing foreign law experts to be assisted by medico-legal experts when compiling their reports, their reports would incorporate material outside of their expertise that the expert would not be able to properly address in cross-examination.

[72] Regulation EC No 846/2007 on the law applicable to non-contractual obligations.

Despite the decision in *Wall*, the reality of what this decision means on the ground is somewhat complicated. Practitioners may have difficulties with their foreign experts insisting that they cannot complete their report on quantum (or indeed cannot opine on aspects of it) without the assistance of a medico-legal expert. For example, a French lawyer may say that they cannot give an opinion about what the consolidation date is in respect of the claimant's injuries because they are not medically qualified.

How can you get around this in practice? It is not unusual to see reference in a claimant or a defendant's budget or directions at a CCMC stage to costings for medico-legal experts. A party may even provide some evidence from the expert to say that the involvement of a medico-legal practitioner is essential. The problem with this approach is that it flies in the face of *Wall*, thus it is rarely successful. A more pragmatic approach is to get the English medical experts to provide answers to a number of questions that the foreign law expert needs to be answered, so that the expert can complete their report. It may well be the case (with some convincing and discussion of how the legal system operates in this jurisdiction in this respect) that the foreign expert is eventually able to feel comfortable giving an opinion on these issues in their role as an expert.

Experts giving evidence at trial

Should your experts need to give evidence at trial, it is important to bear in mind Annex 3 of Practice Direction 32 if it is anticipated they will attend remotely from a foreign jurisdiction.[73] It cannot be presumed that foreign governments will be willing to allow either their own nationals, or individuals present in their jurisdiction, to give

73 See Volume 1 of the White Book (2022).

evidence remotely to an English court. Should a party wish for their expert to give evidence remotely from abroad, enquiries must be made with the FCDO to ensure that the country in question does not raise any objection to it. Permission to give evidence may need to be obtained from the local courts.

Where there is a pre-trial review, a party should have obtained any necessary permission by the date of the pre-trial review and should inform the court of the outcome.[74] If there is no pre-trial review, permission should be obtained by the time of filing the pre-trial checklist and should be recorded in the checklist itself.[75]

---

74 See paragraph 2 of 'Practice Note: Witnesses Giving Evidence Remotely', Sir Julian Flaux (2021).

75 Ibid, paragraph 3.

CHAPTER NINE

CONTRIBUTION CLAIMS

A situation may arise where a claimant has surgery or treatment in England or Wales, following which they are dissatisfied with their outcome. As such, they may seek to have 'corrective' treatment abroad. In some circumstances, this 'corrective' treatment could be argued to have worsened their outcome, rather than to have improved it. If a claimant later brings proceedings against their treatment provider in England and Wales (such as the NHS, for example), the treatment provider may wish to consider bringing a contribution claim.

In such a scenario, a defendant may wish to bring a Part 20 claim against the foreign surgeon/clinic, asking for a contribution or indemnity under the Civil Liability (Contribution) Act 1978 ("the 1978 Act"). This chapter discusses how such a claim may work in practice.

Contribution claims

Section 1(1) of the 1978 Act makes plain that a defendant will need to demonstrate that a foreign surgeon/clinic is liable in respect of the same damage. This will be more complicated than in those clinical negligence cases that do not have a cross-border element. The defendant will need to consider what the applicable law is in relation to that foreign surgical treatment, as well as the potential need to obtain an expert report setting out that the foreign surgeon/clinic is liable. Defendants should be alive to this issue early on in litigation, as issues may arise in respect of the length of time it may take to obtain a foreign expert report, as well as in respect of limitation.

Limitation

Practitioners should be fully alive to section 1(3) of the 1978 Act when considering a contribution claim in cross-border clinical negligence proceedings. The effect of section 1(3) is that a potential defendant can resist a contribution claim if the expiry of limitation period has the effect of extinguishing the claimant's right of action against them (rather than barring it). By way of an example, if a claimant had surgical treatment in Turkey that exacerbated the injuries they sustained following treatment under the NHS and proceeded to sue the NHS, an NHS trust may wish to bring contribution proceedings against the Turkish surgeon and/or clinic. If Turkish law applies[76], the trust will need to obtain an expert report to comment on the limitation period under Turkish law and whether the claimant's cause of action would be extinguished following the expiration of that period. If the limitation period has expired under Turkish law and the cause of action has been extinguished, a contribution claim will not get off the ground.

Does the 1978 Act have overriding effect?

The Supreme Court recently considered the effect of the 1978 Act in the case of *The Soldiers, Sailors, Airmen and Families Association – Forces Help and another (Respondents) v Allgemeines Krankenhauys Viersen GmbH (Appellant).*[77] In *Soldiers*, the claimant was born in a German hospital, which was operated by a third party (*Allgemeines*). During the course of his birth, he suffered an acute hypoxic brain injury. A claim was brought on his behalf in England against the

---

[76] See Chapter Six for a detailed discussion of applicable law.

[77] *The Soldiers, Sailors, Airmen and Families Association – Forces Help and another v Allgemeines Krankenhaus Viersen GmbH* [2022] UKSC 29 (SC).

charity which supplied the midwife (namely SSAFA) and the Ministry of Defence (who indemnified SSAFA), alleging that the midwife's negligence caused his brain damage, for which both defendants were vicariously liable. The defendants denied liability and issued a CPR Part 20 claim against the German hospital, seeking a contribution under section 1 of the 1978 Act.

It was common ground between the parties that the claimant's claim against the defendants was governed by German law and that any liability of the third party was also governed by German law. The parties also agreed that German law would apply to the contribution claim.

The key issue was in respect of the interpretation of the 1978 Act. Under German law, limitation in respect of the Part 20 claim had expired. The defendants argued that the 1978 Act had overriding effect (i.e., that the 1978 Act mandated the application of English law to issues which would otherwise be governed by a foreign law), which meant that limitation was governed by section 10 of the Limitation Act 1980 and the contribution claim was therefore not time barred.

The Court of Appeal held that the 1978 Act did have overriding effect and applied irrespective of domestic choice of law rules. The Supreme Court, however, took a different view. Lord Lloyd-Jones (with whom the other lord justices agreed) considered that the 1978 Act did not expressly provide that it had overriding effect. There was no provision that the 1978 Act applied irrespective of the foreign law that was otherwise applicable to the contribution claim. The Supreme Court considered that the 1978 Act was not intended to have overriding effect so as to displace conventional choice of law rules.

The impact of SSAFA

Where does the Supreme Court's decision leave us? In essence, where the law applicable to the contribution claim is not English law, foreign law will apply to liability, quantum, and limitation in respect of the contribution claim. If a contribution claim against a third party fails, the costs consequences that will follow are that the defendant will have to pay the third party's costs.[78]

[78] See *Wagenaar v Weekend Travel Ltd (t/a Ski Weekend)* [2014] EWCA Civ 1105 (CA).

CHAPTER TEN

QUANTUM

When considering quantum in a cross-border clinical negligence claim, practitioners must bear in mind that the quantum that may be awarded by the court depends on what law applies to the claim. What may sound ordinarily in English damages, may not sound in foreign law.

What if English law applies to the claim?

If you are dealing with a claim where English law applies, you can proceed to quantify the claim as you ordinarily would for any domestic clinical negligence claim and utilise *Facts & Figures*[79] and *Kemp*[80] for special damages as usual. There will be no difference in how quantum is determined. The schedule of loss and counter-schedule will continue to be pleaded in accordance with English law, as will the interest claimed. There will be no reason to seek recourse from a foreign law expert to assist with assessing the applicable damages.

What if foreign law applies to the claim?

If foreign law applies to the claim, matters can be somewhat more complicated. The foreign law experts will need to comment on how

---

79 *Facts & Figures 2022/2023* (September 2022), William Latimer-Sayer KC and ors.

80 *Kemp & Kemp: Quantum of Damages* (August 2022), William Norris KC and ors.

quantum is assessed under foreign law, as well as what is (and what is not) recoverable. Any schedule of loss or counter-schedule will need to accurately set out what damages are claimed, and under which law they are claimed.

Quantum could be far more or far less generous under foreign law than it is under English law. It may be, for example, that foreign law does not allow for the recovery of a claim for care, which may dramatically decrease what that aspect of the claim would ordinarily be worth under English law. On the other hand, bereavement damages in other jurisdictions are often quantified far more generously than under the law in England and Wales.

In light of the above, it is dangerous to assume that English law will always give rise to a far more advantageous result for claimants. If you are for a claimant, it is therefore worth quantifying any claim under both English law and any potential applicable foreign law, so as to determine which law is the more advantageous to the client. It is also pertinent for defendant practitioners to consider this issue, particularly where the parties contest which law applies to the claim, so that they can warn their clients as to how damages may vary depending upon what law is found to apply to the claim.

What if the experts reach different conclusions?

Both parties' experts may reach very different conclusions on what the appropriate level of quantum is in a particular case. Often in these claims, when looking at the foreign law equivalent to general damages, reference will be made by experts to the date upon which the injuries consolidate. The experts may disagree as to when consolidation precisely took place. If the experts do reach opposing positions, their evidence will likely need to be tested at trial.

Sometimes, an expert may reach a particular date of consolidation of the basis of an assumption as to when the claimant reached a certain point in their recovery. Parties should look carefully at the evidence (including not just the medical reports, but the treatment, GP and hospital records, as well as the claimant's witness statement) to see if the expert's reasoning as to the date of consolidation accords with that evidence. If it does not, there may be a basis to argue that the expert in question has underestimated or overestimated when the date of consolidation was.

When looking at special damages under foreign law, there is often a far greater degree of agreement between the parties' experts. The experts do not usually disagree as to whether a head of damage is recoverable or not. However, the foreign law may require that the head of damage is only recoverable if evidenced by receipts, invoices or the like.

Consideration should also be given to the fact that some foreign jurisdictions do not routinely award future special damages to claimants. In some jurisdictions, future damages will only be awarded when it is certain that they will occur and if the amount is clearly determinable at the time of the conclusion of the proceedings. If it is not certain that the damages will occur and the costs are not determinable at that time, the damages will be covered by a declaratory judgment and can be claimed in the future if and when they actually do occur. As one might expect in these claims, it is often not possible to predict with any certainty that a future loss will definitely occur, which may result in a claimant receiving a smaller damages award.

Interest

Following *Wall v Mutuelle*, whilst foreign law may apply to a claim, English law will govern the rules of evidence and procedure.[81] Recent authorities have considered that interest is a procedural, rather than a substantive, matter. As such, the interest rates that may be awarded to a claimant may be those of the lex fori, i.e., under the Senior Courts Act 1981 or County Courts Act 1984. Whether or not a substantive right to interest under foreign law exists, the English courts have a discretion to decide whether to award interest and to determine the relevant amount.[82] It may be however that in a claim governed by foreign applicable law, the court will decide to exercise its discretion in favour of the utilising foreign rates of interest. In some jurisdictions the applicable rate can be as high as 20%, which can lead to interest becoming a head of loss of significant value in and of itself. In all cases involving foreign applicable law, consideration should be given as to whether applying foreign rates of interest gives rise to an advantageous result to the client. Should a party wish to seek to persuade a court to utilise a foreign interest rate, expert evidence as to what that rate is will need to be obtained.

---

81 *Wall v Mutuelle de Poitiers Assurances* [2014] EWCA Civ 138 (CA).

82 *Maher and another v Groupana Grand Est* [2009] EWCA Civ [2010] 1 WLR 1564.

MORE BOOKS BY LAW BRIEF PUBLISHING

A selection of our other titles available now:-

'A Practical Guide to Parental Alienation in Private and Public Law Children Cases' by Sam King QC & Frankie Shama
'Contested Heritage – Removing Art from Land and Historic Buildings' by Richard Harwood QC, Catherine Dobson, David Sawtell
'The Limits of Separate Legal Personality: When Those Running a Company Can Be Held Personally Liable for Losses Caused to Third Parties Outside of the Company' by Dr Mike Wilkinson
'A Practical Guide to Transgender Law' by Robin Moira White & Nicola Newbegin
'Artificial Intelligence – The Practical Legal Issues (2nd Edition)' by John Buyers
'A Practical Guide to Residential Freehold Conveyancing' by Lorraine Richardson
'A Practical Guide to Pensions on Divorce for Lawyers' by Bryan Scant
'A Practical Guide to Challenging Sham Marriage Allegations in Immigration Law' by Priya Solanki
'A Practical Guide to Legal Rights in Scotland' by Sarah-Jane Macdonald
'A Practical Guide to New Build Conveyancing' by Paul Sams & Rebecca East
'A Practical Guide to Defending Barristers in Disciplinary Cases' by Marc Beaumont
'A Practical Guide to Inherited Wealth on Divorce' by Hayley Trim
'A Practical Guide to Practice Direction 12J and Domestic Abuse in Private Law Children Proceedings' by Rebecca Cross & Malvika Jaganmohan
'A Practical Guide to Confiscation and Restraint' by Narita Bahra QC, John Carl Townsend, David Winch
'A Practical Guide to the Law of Forests in Scotland' by Philip Buchan
'A Practical Guide to Health and Medical Cases in Immigration Law' by Rebecca Chapman & Miranda Butler
'A Practical Guide to Bad Character Evidence for Criminal Practitioners by Aparna Rao
'A Practical Guide to Extradition Law post-Brexit' by Myles Grandison et al

'A Practical Guide to Hoarding and Mental Health for Housing Lawyers' by Rachel Coyle
'A Practical Guide to Psychiatric Claims in Personal Injury – 2nd Edition' by Liam Ryan
'Stephens on Contractual Indemnities' by Richard Stephens
'A Practical Guide to the EU Succession Regulation' by Richard Frimston
'A Practical Guide to Solicitor and Client Costs – 2nd Edition' by Robin Dunne
'Constructive Dismissal – Practice Pointers and Principles' by Benjimin Burgher
'A Practical Guide to Religion and Belief Discrimination Claims in the Workplace' by Kashif Ali
'A Practical Guide to the Law of Medical Treatment Decisions' by Ben Troke
'Fundamental Dishonesty and QOCS in Personal Injury Proceedings: Law and Practice' by Jake Rowley
'A Practical Guide to the Law in Relation to School Exclusions' by Charlotte Hadfield & Alice de Coverley
'A Practical Guide to Divorce for the Silver Separators' by Karin Walker
'The Right to be Forgotten – The Law and Practical Issues' by Melissa Stock
'A Practical Guide to Planning Law and Rights of Way in National Parks, the Broads and AONBs' by James Maurici QC, James Neill et al
'A Practical Guide to Election Law' by Tom Tabori
'A Practical Guide to the Law in Relation to Surrogacy' by Andrew Powell
'A Practical Guide to Claims Arising from Fatal Accidents – 2nd Edition' by James Patience
'A Practical Guide to the Ownership of Employee Inventions – From Entitlement to Compensation' by James Tumbridge & Ashley Roughton
'A Practical Guide to Asbestos Claims' by Jonathan Owen & Gareth McAloon
'A Practical Guide to Stamp Duty Land Tax in England and Northern Ireland' by Suzanne O'Hara
'A Practical Guide to the Law of Farming Partnerships' by Philip Whitcomb
'Covid-19, Homeworking and the Law – The Essential Guide to Employment and GDPR Issues' by Forbes Solicitors
'Covid-19 and Criminal Law – The Essential Guide' by Ramya Nagesh
'Covid-19 and Family Law in England and Wales – The Essential Guide' by Safda Mahmood

'A Practical Guide to the Law of Unlawful Eviction and Harassment – 2nd Edition' by Stephanie Lovegrove
'Covid-19, Brexit and the Law of Commercial Leases – The Essential Guide' by Mark Shelton
'A Practical Guide to Costs in Personal Injury Claims – 2nd Edition' by Matthew Hoe
'A Practical Guide to the General Data Protection Regulation (GDPR) – 2nd Edition' by Keith Markham
'Ellis on Credit Hire – Sixth Edition' by Aidan Ellis & Tim Kevan
'A Practical Guide to Working with Litigants in Person and McKenzie Friends in Family Cases' by Stuart Barlow
'Protecting Unregistered Brands: A Practical Guide to the Law of Passing Off' by Lorna Brazell
'A Practical Guide to Secondary Liability and Joint Enterprise Post-Jogee' by Joanne Cecil & James Mehigan
'A Practical Guide to the Pre-Action RTA Claims Protocol for Personal Injury Lawyers' by Antonia Ford
'A Practical Guide to Neighbour Disputes and the Law' by Alexander Walsh
'A Practical Guide to Forfeiture of Leases' by Mark Shelton
'A Practical Guide to Coercive Control for Legal Practitioners and Victims' by Rachel Horman
'A Practical Guide to Rights Over Airspace and Subsoil' by Daniel Gatty
'Tackling Disclosure in the Criminal Courts – A Practitioner's Guide' by Narita Bahra QC & Don Ramble
'A Practical Guide to the Law of Driverless Cars – Second Edition' by Alex Glassbrook, Emma Northey & Scarlett Milligan
'A Practical Guide to TOLATA Claims' by Greg Williams
'A Practical Guide to Elderly Law – 2nd Edition' by Justin Patten
'A Practical Guide to Responding to Housing Disrepair and Unfitness Claims' by Iain Wightwick
'A Practical Guide to the Construction and Rectification of Wills and Trust Instruments' by Edward Hewitt
'A Practical Guide to the Law of Bullying and Harassment in the Workplace' by Philip Hyland
'How to Be a Freelance Solicitor: A Practical Guide to the SRA-Regulated Freelance Solicitor Model' by Paul Bennett

'A Practical Guide to Prison Injury Claims' by Malcolm Johnson
'A Practical Guide to the Small Claims Track - 2nd Edition' by Dominic Bright
'A Practical Guide to Advising Clients at the Police Station' by Colin Stephen McKeown-Beaumont
'A Practical Guide to Antisocial Behaviour Injunctions' by Iain Wightwick
'Practical Mediation: A Guide for Mediators, Advocates, Advisers, Lawyers, and Students in Civil, Commercial, Business, Property, Workplace, and Employment Cases' by Jonathan Dingle with John Sephton
'The Mini-Pupillage Workbook' by David Boyle
'A Practical Guide to Crofting Law' by Brian Inkster
'A Practical Guide to Spousal Maintenance' by Liz Cowell
'A Practical Guide to the Law of Domain Names and Cybersquatting' by Andrew Clemson
'A Practical Guide to the Law of Gender Pay Gap Reporting' by Harini Iyengar
'A Practical Guide to the Rights of Grandparents in Children Proceedings' by Stuart Barlow
'NHS Whistleblowing and the Law' by Joseph England
'Employment Law and the Gig Economy' by Nigel Mackay & Annie Powell
'A Practical Guide to Noise Induced Hearing Loss (NIHL) Claims' by Andrew Mckie, Ian Skeate, Gareth McAloon
'An Introduction to Beauty Negligence Claims – A Practical Guide for the Personal Injury Practitioner' by Greg Almond
'Intercompany Agreements for Transfer Pricing Compliance' by Paul Sutton
'Zen and the Art of Mediation' by Martin Plowman
'A Practical Guide to the SRA Principles, Individual and Law Firm Codes of Conduct 2019 – What Every Law Firm Needs to Know' by Paul Bennett
'A Practical Guide to Adoption for Family Lawyers' by Graham Pegg
'A Practical Guide to Industrial Disease Claims' by Andrew Mckie & Ian Skeate
'A Practical Guide to Redundancy' by Philip Hyland
'A Practical Guide to Vicarious Liability' by Mariel Irvine
'A Practical Guide to Applications for Landlord's Consent and Variation of Leases' by Mark Shelton
'A Practical Guide to Relief from Sanctions Post-Mitchell and Denton' by Peter Causton

'A Practical Guide to Equity Release for Advisors' by Paul Sams
'A Practical Guide to Financial Services Claims' by Chris Hegarty
'The Law of Houses in Multiple Occupation: A Practical Guide to HMO Proceedings' by Julian Hunt
'Occupiers, Highways and Defective Premises Claims: A Practical Guide Post-Jackson – 2nd Edition' by Andrew Mckie
'A Practical Guide to Financial Ombudsman Service Claims' by Adam Temple & Robert Scrivenor
'A Practical Guide to Advising Schools on Employment Law' by Jonathan Holden
'A Practical Guide to Running Housing Disrepair and Cavity Wall Claims: 2nd Edition' by Andrew Mckie & Ian Skeate
'A Practical Guide to Holiday Sickness Claims – 2nd Edition' by Andrew Mckie & Ian Skeate
'Arguments and Tactics for Personal Injury and Clinical Negligence Claims' by Dorian Williams
'A Practical Guide to Drone Law' by Rufus Ballaster, Andrew Firman, Eleanor Clot
'A Practical Guide to Compliance for Personal Injury Firms Working With Claims Management Companies' by Paul Bennett
'RTA Allegations of Fraud in a Post-Jackson Era: The Handbook – 2nd Edition' by Andrew Mckie
'RTA Personal Injury Claims: A Practical Guide Post-Jackson' by Andrew Mckie
'On Experts: CPR35 for Lawyers and Experts' by David Boyle
'An Introduction to Personal Injury Law' by David Boyle

www.ingramcontent.com/pod-product-compliance
Ingram Content Group UK Ltd.
Pitfield, Milton Keynes, MK11 3LW, UK
UKHW020151290926
15471UKWH00004B/804

9 781914 608636